SPRING BIRTH *and Other Poems*

MARK VAN DOREN

SPRING

BIRTH

and

Other Poems

HENRY HOLT AND COMPANY
Publishers   *New York*

The author wishes to thank the following magazines and newspapers for permission to reprint the poems which they first published: Bayonne (N. J.) *Times, Commentary, Good Housekeeping, Harper's Magazine, Hobart Review, Hopkins Review, Kenyon Review, Ladies' Home Journal,* Lakeville (Conn.) *Journal, The Nation, Olivet Quarterly, Park East, St. John's Collegian, Saturday Review of Literature, Sewanee Review, Virginia Quarterly Review, Wake, Woman's Home Companion.* "Single Majesty" and "Edge of Town: Indiana" appeared originally in *The New Yorker.* The contents of two pamphlets are reprinted in this volume with the kind permission of their publishers: *Humanity Unlimited, Twelve Sonnets,* College of William and Mary, Williamsburg, Virginia, 1950; and *In That Far Land,* The Prairie Press, Iowa City, Iowa, 1951.

Copyright, 1953, by Mark Van Doren

First Edition

Library of Congress Catalog Card Number: 52-13076

Printed in the United States of America

To

Dorothy

Contents

SONNETS

THE PEOPLE OF THE WORD

DEATH WENT AWAY

The Bird Desire

I Went, I Saw

I went, I saw, but will not tell,
But cannot tell, what things were there.
They are not here; but even so,
There is this difference of air.

Excitement then, like spicy smoke,
Invisible, yet followed me.
It curled among the corridors,
It burned above the hills, the sea.

No person's eyes that looked in mine,
No woman's, but a pepper scent
Filled room and street and blowing field;
And nosegay children came and went;

And animals, so pure of coat
They glistened in that sleeker sun—
But where this was I will not tell,
Nor things I did there—no, not one.

Because You Go with Me

All women are beautiful,
All men are brave,
Because you go with me
This side the grave;
Because the same shadows
That I see and fear
Shorten before you
And disappear.

All women are beautiful
Because you are one;
All the world's courage—
But I have none—
All the day's splendor
Springs out of you.
Even I, knowing it,
Am carefree too.

Even I, dangling
The sun at my side,
Sometimes can wonder
If those shadows lied
That said they were longer
Because of my doubt;
So deep, my darling,
You burn it out.

My Poor Love

Keep up your humming, west wind, and your silly
Songs, you birds; and all you trees, half bent
With sound, keep whispering to the grass, the ground.

Keep noisy, world; yet leave one little crack
For silence to slip through you, one thin cleft,
One hollow vein that my poor love can follow.

My poor love, it cannot cry—not loud
It cannot, nor so sweet as those small sparrows,
Piping, nor so warm as her eyes, weeping.

There she waits—oh, I know where—and truly
Listens—O my love, she truly leans
And listens; for my silence here she listens.

Let it go then, wind and thunder, let it
Pass between you, songbirds, let it pierce you,
Trees, like words upon the wing—oh, these.

She Lives with Me

She lives with me and is my careless love;
All of my faults are funny in her heart.
All of her faults—but she has buried those;
I cannot find them with my fondest art.

I watch and pry, and have a name for one,
Should it be ever proven and confessed:
There is no dark religion in her love;
I am not God, but a forgiven guest.

My faults are foibles, like my very strength;
My deepest virtue she indulges too.
I am not terrible to see and hear;
My work is play that curious children do.

She lives with me and is my laughing love,
Nor would I have it different in her mind.
Her single sin—but it is never so,
Nor could I wish it any sweeter kind.

Let Me Not See

Let me not see the one I love,
The bright one, that so blinded me;
The sweet one, that like sudden roses
Filled all evening easterly.
Let me not have those senses back
That sleep in her, and only lack
Knowledge of their captivity.

They think they are awake in me
And working, as they did of old.
And still they do with her away;
Then everything is clear and cold;
Is single, and I hear its name.
Oh, let it never be the same
With her whom clouds of love enfold.

She comes, but not herself is there.
She moves, but in a mist I make.
Oh, let me never burn away
All this between us, for love's sake.
Let my desire be even such
As darkens most what then I touch—
Sudden midnight, and fireflake.

The Liquid Heart

What if it is happening now—
Even now—the slow drain,
The drying, drying, drying up—
Oh, what if even now the gods
Go elsewhere in the joyful night?

They lay with me, and when I rose
They would not leave my happy side—
Unhappy too, but oh, how sweet
My bitterness was then, how full—
They lived with me and were my love.

Together we made worlds and worlds,
By night, by day, and none was calm,
And none, save at the center, clear.
Not one but was our changeling child
Whom only I must then subdue.

Yet now that I am master thus,
Where do those tall companions range?
I know, I know. The liquid heart
They lie with there—were it my own,
I would not for this world be wise.

The Bird Desire

I took my gun,
I walked a mile,
And shot and killed
The bird desire.

Still it flew.
I shot again.
It fell to ground.
Desire was dead.

What then is this
That dips so near,
And on not two
But twenty wings?

No, a hundred.
Thousands now.
Where shall I hide?
Should I be proud?

I gave a mortal
Thing this life.
I made a god.
He multiplies.

Goddess of the Gown

The huge world of thighs that silk and cotton
And the smooth wool conceal—how would it be,
O custom, if your curtain fell away
One day,
O custom, and it worked as waves work,
Openly, on, on, and on,
To the eye's limit, to the thinking end?

That wilderness of soft and moving monsters,
Those riders of the plain—how would it be,
O mythical sweet art, if you resigned,
And the slow mind,
O mythical sweet seamstress, quickened;
If sleepiness in dogs and men
Gave way to round and rolling wonder?

The forests of them then the sun perfumed!
Or, spicily in rooms, the overflowing—
O hider of all that, would you return?
We burn,
O cunning cover, as it is, in dream.
Could we do more—could we as much—
Goddess, if no silk assisted?

Hector Dead

Andromache, when Hector fell,
Cried out upon her fate, not his.
He lost but this one thing, the world;
She gained its million miseries.

Without him it was no more round
And perfect, as pure death can be.
A field of wry-shaped fragments wailed,
Each one of them sharp-voiced as she.

A wilderness of woes it was
By which she measured, that long day,
The quietness in his great throat
That once held every dog away.

Home Eagerly

Home eagerly to give the gift,
The single thing bought on this day
In the whole world for that lone one.

That one who pays by keeping there
The room you come to, and herself
Is lone receiver, cord and box.

Which now unwrapping, nevertheless
Remember. It was giving more
To stay and open this white door.

As Time Goes On

As time goes on, and tells us less
And less what we have language for,
Still we converse; that vacuum
Is something still we must abhor.

As mind lives on, and feeds itself
With self, yet cannot name the taste,
Still we conceive; there is a world
Inside us that we may not waste.

As joy survives despite despair,
And yet despair declines to die,
Still we consent; it is our lot
To love without good reason why.

In That Far Land

Only for Me

When I was twelve in that far land,
And was in love with summer nights,
And was in love with Linda Jane,
Whose very name was dancing lights
About my dark, my country bed,
Once I dreamed that she was dead.

And woke; and not one window star,
As I looked out, but wept for me.
I looked again, and my own tears,
Like magic lanterns, made me see
The very eyes of Linda Jane
Weeping everywhere like rain.

Then the sunrise, cool and red,
And then the new day, white and hot.
And after that the growing up
And the forgetting—oh, but not
The selfless woe of one that died.
Only for me, for me she cried.

Neighborhood Enough

The mind at last fills up with men
Whom infant thought found wonderful:
The next-door men that made the world
So curious, so multiple.

Then down the street the stranger ones,
And on and on to millions more;
But these alone were universe,
Were firmament and fiery shore.

The talk of them was news enough,
And when they died, was history.
The simple purpose of the sun
Was that they were and still should be.

And still they are, without their names,
Next door to memory grown old;
When further stars are faint to see,
And all between is dark and cold.

The little world is warm again,
Is numerous, and windows blink;
And men within, obscure as mice,
Make neighborhood enough, we think.

Homer, Sidney, Philo

Homer, Sidney, Philo,
Strung along the Wabash:
Beads in the black land.
Corn grows, but no change
In these little towns.

After forty springtimes
Nothing to look out at.
Seven miles, eight miles—
Strangers in the blue express
Yawn and despise them.

So would I, certainly,
Except that I remember
Homer Park on hot days.
We took the interurban.
We kissed in the shade.

Sidney was our junction;
Six trains a week there.
We rode the dusty local—
Opening all windows—
Then to Detroit.

Philo we drove through,
Cold nights, with horses.
Once there was a dim lamp
Showing, and my father
Stopped for oyster stew.

After forty autumns,
Only I am different.
Here they are as always;
They cannot remember
Themselves as I do.

Spring Birth

The lord of increase, traveling with me,
Said: "Look! There are more than you will see,
Yet look!" And laughed, and pointed at the small
Pigs bouncing as they ran, and at the tall
Bewildered foals, their four legs wildly braced
Lest the ground heave again; while kittens chased
White butterflies, and calves, all ears and head,
Butted and sucked as their great mothers fed.
The lord of increase grinned. "A few of mine,
With foster-help. But listen!" And the whine
Of mayflies filled my ears, and far away,
In wilderness, eggs opened unto day,
And little serpents—were they noiseless?—slid
Through the warm sand. Bare birds above them hid,
Faint-peeping, and a hornet lifted wing
For the first time in nature—not to sting,
But trying the blue air. "All these, and more.
Now close your eyelids." And the forest floor
Padded with feet of foxes, old and young,
As ugly owlets blinked, and beetles clung
To ridges of last winter's bark. "More yet?"
But I believed him, lord of all beget.

Edge of Town: Indiana

Windy spring wakes color up.
See? The green blood returns, and stains
Hedges and hills; and wanton meadows
Wave at the windows of great trains.

Not here, though; the black engine halts
By houses that keep winter time.
This weatherboarding will not bloom,
Whatever happens in May prime.

Whatever comes by upper air—
See? The high trees: their secret flowers!—
These dun verandahs will not flush
With excess joy like ours, like ours.

Like ours. Except the last one there—
Look! The clean curtains, red and white.
And who is this young woman bending
In the green breeze, and pulling tight

The string he plants by? Straight the rows,
Straight the backs of two that stand,
Suddenly, and smile at us,
Leaving them to their sweet land.

The Merry Trainman

Apologetic, the old person in the black hat
Fumbles to descend, saying: "Once I could do this
    faster."
"Can't fool me," fellow in the blue cap answers.
    "Dancing,
Dancing—you was up all night—I know it—dancing!
Shame on all such girls. Where's Henry?" And the grand-
    child
Jumps from the top step of the vestibule—clear down—
And clings. "Old-timer! Well! Hello! And how is crops?"
They both go comforted. He tilts his dusty cap.
"Indianapolis local! Last chance this morning
To visit the state capital and bring back home
Some silver souvenirs. What's that? Three quarters of a
    half hour
Late? Not by the sun"—he squints—"but what if so?
Who hurries, and who worries? Up with you, Tom
    Carson.
Smoking car on the right. But I don't recommend it.
Board! All aboard!" And the coach, creaking among
    cornfields,
Bears on the summer rails his chosen people, smiling.
Seat by sleepy seat he ministers, this Mercury,
This clown of the blue cloth, while overhead the high
    planes
Hum, with kings in them, or queens for all he cares.

Path Out of Town

No way is straight, so this one wanders
As the first mind did, and the feet,
Obedient, that bending wove,
In the still grass, thought's little street.

And no one since but absently
Winds likewise; not the lover's will,
Not the thief's haste, but history
Determines how we take the hill.

Or is it more, and natural:
Necessity in every curve?
The old man coming with his basket—
He will not hesitate to swerve

As the ground swings, upholding him
For the last time perhaps he fears.
The blind wife, bearing lunch to field,
Touches her dog's attentive ears

And sings, for now the way is sure,
The serpent way some first one found:
Commendable to man and girl;
Commodious for wind and hound.

To Be on Trains

To be on trains, perfection of alone:
The one among the many that the blue cap
Counts not, sitting in the roar
Of such a startled stillness as the whistle—
Where?—unmakes and makes as whirlwinds do
Necessity of sound. To be this one
Yet no one that the blue cap, bending, sees.
To be nowhere but here, and yet not, yet not
Anywhere by night, by day—which is it,
Brother in the green seat opposite, sister
Ahead there, swimming under time's
Thick water, under firmaments of—oh,
To be and not be numbered—let it go
Oh, anywhere, this absolute alone.

Civilization

Before the eaves stop dripping, there they are,
Those martins. They come out of doors and sit.
They shake off showery drops. They almost hold
A hand out, testing the sun's intention.
One of them, in shirtsleeves, reconsiders
Darkness; but his neighbor treads the porch,
Looks right and left for enemies, looks up;
Looks down; and—what no man could do—dives,
Dives, and comes back up with a bent twig
That disappears with him as dead grass does
A busy minute later; when more birds,
On the north side, near where the thunder was,
Issue and sit, reflective; then decide
And fly, and fill the air all afternoon
With comings and with goings; and between,
The looking down. They say this little city
On the high pole is theirs, and that they built it.
Better for them than the poor hollow trees
Their first parents fashioned—all those tops
That tossed, and bark that rotted; and the squirrel teeth
That chattered. None of these but can remember,
Gazing east, the wilderness that was.

In Douglas County

In Douglas County winds do blow—
No doubt of it—all night, all day.
And did long since. My grandchild cheek
Itself remembers, in dry May,

How the first men here, setting forth,
Took their own faces for a guide.
Where the wind struck, on eye or temple—
That was southwest, and would abide.

So off they journeyed—green the waste,
And sometimes flowery, but no trees;
No tell-tale tops to mark the land:
Compasses for throats and knees.

Nothing but this that must not shift;
Southwest was here where the forehead stung.
One man was lost. But I believe
The whole high world that morning swung.

What Fury

What fury in the white sky
Showing over Shepherd's woods!
Look! Is it a kingbird
Or purple martin pouncing so?
There! He almost had the duck hawk
Down. But then he let him go.

Courage? Would you call it that?
Spirit, in a speck as wild
As windy leaf, as falling flake?
Now the updraft—see him rise
And give it to him hard again—
Always aiming at the eyes.

Wrath? Or is it even felt?
Rage at least would have a reason.
Where in such a little brain—
But it is finished. There he went.
He was only playing blazes
In blue air. A spark, and spent.

Single Majesty

Behold him, that great solitary
Tree in the forgotten field.
Fences, falling, left him long ago
To lord it, and he does,
That archer,
That great reacher oak,
That master of this meadow, bent
By nothing but strong wind.
No fellow crowds him,
Nothing but the sun on all sides
Shapes him—oh, so full
That crown, as if no other lord
Lived anywhere, no grass
But waited for this shadow,
No birds were
But his.
Behold him and forget him if you can,
That king
Of this lost meadow.

The Only World

The meadow hedge hides meadowlarks
Whose voices rise as rise the roses,
Breaking at the top in bloom
Of sound and scent while daytime dozes;

Dozes over wind and dust;
Dozes over tractor roar—
Behemoth of the middle world
Murders music more and more.

Yet here by hedge the hidden throat,
The buried thorn decline the death;
Sending bubbles up and up
Of sweetly broken heart and breath

Till every leaf is overlaid,
Till every drop of air is drowned,
And sleepy daytime dreams again
Of its own scent, of its own sound.

This is the only world that was;
That will be when Behemoth dies;
That is at all, the meadowlarks
And roses murmur as they rise.

Culture of Corn

The great machines that mouse these fields
In May, between the long, dark showers—
How they do master and despise
The stick, the hoe that once were ours.

Even the coulter, tearing sod,
Even the horses, our huge slaves—
The red machines remember nothing.
Man and beast are in their graves,

And only metal that moves itself
Goes back and forth here, biting in.
Yet truth to say, the softened fields,
Supine, are willing that it win.

They lie there, those great breeding queens,
Brown at the breast and cool of womb,
And wait for seed; nor ever sigh
Because no two feet, four feet come.

Granary

The tall new crib is woven steel:
A humming cylinder in wind—
This wind—that once on weathered boards
Stopped dead. It made no music then,
Nor knows perhaps it whispers now
Among the meshes of such walls.

So high it is, so huge and old,
It may not hear what things it does,
It may not care if wood or wire,
If buildings, if October trees,
Stand out of earth a little way,
Opposing it a little while.

Come closer. Listen, and look up.
The whole sky—does it seem to sound?
But let your memory climb too,
And spread and spread till this is gone.
What did we say? Did something sing?
Does corn still blossom? Are there men?

The Uncle I Was Named For

The uncle I was named for
Is not there now, four muddy miles
Northwest of Wapanucka, Oklahoma.
But I remember 1939.
"Ask anyone in town how to get out here."
I had the letter, and I asked
At the first filling station.
"Mark Butz? Believe I seen him."
"Where?" "Oh, down a ways."
And so I started, but was stopped almost at once
By a fat person in loose overalls.
"Are you Mark Butz's nephew?"
I didn't need to tell him. "He's in town,
He's looking for you." "Where?"
"Why, could be anywhere. Might try the drugstore."
I hardly got the screen door open. "You
Mark Butz's nephew?" "Yes." "Well, he's been here
All day." "Been where?" "Oh, down a piece.
Been looking for you." "Has he?" I disturbed
The flies again, and started on.
The whole town turned and looked at me,
And waited—oh, they knew—until I came
To the hot awning and the five old men,
And one of them stood up,
The tall one, that my mother named me for.
He's not there now, or anywhere;
Nor has to be, as long as I

Keep on this earth
And can remember.

He went ahead with our own boys,
In an old bronco car that jumped the ruts
Or splashed in them, and laughed
At the worse way I picked as we pursued him;
Then suddenly turned in, uphill a little,
To the squat, square, cement-block house
He had replaced his cabin with,
The log one he lived in as a bachelor.
And that was not so long ago; he married late,
At fifty, and he let the cabin stand
For lumber, or for firewood, off one corner
Of the new porch Aunt Cora waved from.
No log was left now
Of the disorderly old room he had inhabited
Forever, by our legend. A relation
Coming, he would take his shotgun down
And stand in the door and shoot one of his wild
Chickens, and boil it tender in the fireplace.
But that was then. Aunt Cora
Waved, and this was now, and he
Was proud of being different. "Well, get out."
And so we did, for supper in a varnished
Kitchen, under a droplight.
"Your Uncle Mark," she said, "was a hard man
To marry. I had to be a widow first. He wouldn't
Ask me in those other days. In these—
Well, I asked him." And his blue eyes

Were pleased. He was my mother's
Brother, with the same blue eyes; and so we talked
Of her, and Illinois; but not of the time
His father, my grandfather, a little and old
And angry man, disgraced him—sent him off,
I never heard what for. He walked a mile,
Then there was Grandma Butz, come through the oak
     woods
By a short cut. She cried and gave him money.
He didn't know I knew.
"Well, now!" he said, "how long can you be with us?
You didn't really mean it—just one night.
After thirty years, not just one night!"
But so it was. I think he never slept when we did.
I looked out once, and he was reading,
With silver glasses, upright on a cot, still in
His underwear. He wasn't tired,
As we were. Or was excited. Or had sworn
He wouldn't miss our first peep in the morning.
He had of course to wake us up, for pancakes.
"I'll go with you and put you on the good road—
Yes, I will!" insisting. So the boys
Climbed in with him again. Aunt Cora waved
Her apron, and we went; and stopped
When he did, maybe ten slow miles away,
Where the concrete began. Then he got out
And looked at us. "Good-by."
"Good-by." He still could be there,
Looking. He knew it was the last time.
He found it hard to die, Aunt Cora wrote.

No Word, No Wind

What god was there
When the slow buggy, appearing and disappearing,
Slipped in and out of moon and maple shadows, down
Those least of earth's depressions, up those low,
Those prairie rises? Eighteen miles
From town to sleepy town, and not a lamp
In any passing window—oh, so slowly
Passing, as the mare's feet
Shuffled, and the delicate wheels
Answered, invisible in windless
Dust. No weather then,
No breath of any god, no loud intelligence
Looking. Nothing blown out of the north,
No word.
What understanding, nevertheless, what hidden listener
Brooded? For the whole of that great place
Consented—I remember it—
Consented, and we nodded in the narrow
Seat, and safely crawled up hills
That were no hills, down grades that were but folded
Ground, with gentle pockets of cool air
Where the night sighed, considering itself.
No rain, no sun, no sting of snow,
No sound of rivers, sluggish, far away among their syca-
     mores
In bottom land, forgotten.
And no wind.
What god, if nothing breathed? I might go back there,

Maybe, and find out. But that same night
Is not there now;
Never again, I think, will such a stillness
Be, and not be spoken to.
No word, no wind—I swear it,
Not one sign
That the world knew we went that way at all.

II

Whereas in whirling March—oh, I remember—
Or the dog days,
Or knee deep in the Christmas drifts
That crusted later—all white ice
Both ways a thousand miles to where the mountains
        were,
And are, that leave that valley to itself,
Lonesome, and vast, and unreportable—
Or mournfully, in fall,
When the pale corn, suffering the southwest
Trade winds, rustled by night, by day, as if a dead sea
Whispered, pitying the labor
Of its own waves, interminable, intentless—
Then what mind presided? Father
Or mother of all those men,
Those midland children, what lost mind
Like theirs looked down and listened,
Sharing it with them, that great place
To which they both consented? Someone did,
And does. Or are they several, enormous, many-
Minded, with no single
Voice that yet can sing, that yet can say,

As some day it may do, what meaning lies
In the long vacancy between those silent mountains?
So far, not a thoughtful
People; so far, not an articulate
Deity, unless that world of weather
Itself is god, is goddess, trying
Their patience whom alternately it blasts
And lulls to slumber
On hot nights
When grain but not idea grows. I might go back there,
Maybe, and look sharp; and shall,
Some day, and listen. There is no other
Sky that I would rather, after these distant
Years, see face to face.

Sonnets

He Loves Me

That God should love me is more wonderful
Than that I so imperfectly love him.
My reason is mortality, and dim
Senses; his—oh, insupportable—
Is that he sees me. Even when I pull
Dark thoughts about my head, each vein and limb
Delights him, though remembrance in him, grim
With my worst crimes, should prove me horrible.

And he has terrors that he can release.
But when he looks he loves me; which is why
I wonder; and my wonder must increase
Till more of it shall slay me. Yet I live,
I live; and he has never ceased to give
This glance at me that sweetens the whole sky.

Leaves

Past even wondrous flowers—past white and red,
Past the streaked poison petal, strange of name,
Past cups and hanging bells, past wild or tame
Sun-yellow, past bright blue that goes to bed—
Past all of these with whom delight has wed
Since the first dawn moved any to exclaim,
Earth's kingdom loves its leaves, that are the same
Green ever as forever they are fed.

The king himself loves leaves; see how he thrusts
His hoary head among them—heart-shaped things
He fills and fills; for all their veins are his.
See how his breath sleeps in these delicate wings
That never fly away as summer dusts
And dews find out the only world that is.

Between Sunset and Dark

What is it then that beautifies the fields
Between sunset and dark; or soon before,
When the last light and the long shadows pour
So rich a stream, which overflows and builds
Great banks of blossom? Is it death that gilds
Those groves, and that cut grass, outliving more
Than daytime does, than green? Where is the shore
Of all our world, when thus the center yields?

Why is it then that anyone must know?
Enough that now, midway of noon and night,
Suddenly this is. Suddenly cool light,
Caressing its sweet self, turns into dream
These very stones that not so long ago
Were only what tomorrow they will seem.

The Oldest World

The genius of these hills I see in sleep
Chose wisely for himself. They are his rest
From rocks and trees. They roll both east and west,
Barren of all but the smooth shape they keep
As steadily they climb, leaving the deep
Long valley where I lie and count them, lest
One fold of them be gone. They are the best,
The oldest world, before men lived to weep.

The genius of these slopes was jealous then,
And is this night, I know, of stones and groves;
Of wind and tears; of anything upthrust
Or thrashing. Long ago and now again
He herds them, tall and lone. Look how he roves,
Guarding this little earth and my cool dust.

Aftermidsummer

Aftermidsummer, like afternoon,
Suddenly sound-poor, laments the birds
That not so long since, with soprano words,
Shrilled in the trees. And will again, and soon;
They only rest for a hot hour. Their tune,
Up-tumbling, will awake the drowsy herds
In the smooth fields below, as daylight girds
Against the coming sunset and the moon.

The harvest moon, and fall. It is not dark
But cold that comes. Midwinter is the cause,
Far off, that every bird clings to the bark
And listens, letting time tick warm away
As if it were not, and the year, the day,
More perfect for this music in the pause.

A Deer Is Feeding

A deer is feeding in the orchard grass:
A doe; with young ears, maybe, watching her
From the pine thicket southward; not to stir
Until she starts; and then the two will pass,
On amber ankles, delicate as glass,
Among great stones and trees, by dust and burr
Unbothered; or by me—oh, foreigner
Forever, and most terrible, alas.

See how she looks and fears me, all her skin
Atremble. But her eyes—I know them best,
From some that I saw dying once. Within,
How dark, without, how moist. What agony,
What dew of old despair, that even we
Who love them cannot ever burn to rest.

The Keeper and the Kept

The dog indoors, the cat upon the stair,
Four-footed, are at home; and they were so
When other men were here, and the white snow
That fell was not recorded, save as air
Remembers. Wolf and lion, lynx and bear,
And the cold-blooded serpent that must go
Unseen among the rocks, will never know
Of the small beasts that comfort thus our lair.

And satisfy themselves. For wall and rug;
And, past the fender, that unnatural fire,
That sun by night; and milk and meat not dug,
Not wild, but warm in dishes, they accept
As theirs and ours—the keeper and the kept,
And both of us contented with the hire.

Like Raining in a River

Like raining in a river; like the dove,
The mourning dove, when day already dies;
Like dawn at noon were there a sun to rise—
But oh, there is, and she is my own love—
Like dreams in dreams her bounty is, above
All asking, and all wanting, were I wise;
But I am not, and so it multiplies—
My happiness, that nothing will remove.

It is the child of such a sweet excess
In her that loves me, it can never end.
See how she tries, by giving, to be less,
Yet grows; and so my love does, that is friend
To trees and stars, those great ones who confess
All night how far love's limits do extend.

Sullen Love

My grievance that so mounted and so mocked
The very sounds it rose on—where in space,
Between what stars, confirmed in their cold grace,
Does it lie now and sleep, with planets rocked
And great suns soothed and warmed? My wild words
    locked
So long the truth of love in, and my face
So guilty grew, remembering, no near place
Could be their host. But heaven is not shocked.

I still can listen, if I shut my eyes
And shame me, to the falsehood I put forth.
And part believed; the fabricator tries
His best in sullen love to prove the worst.
Faint, though, and far. That anger now is nursed
Only by constellations east and north.

The Mean of Love

"Does he love you?" She hesitated long,
Then listed all the signs of yes and no.
He kept her in his house; but sudden snow
Blew sometimes, and the windows opened wrong.
"Do you love him?" The question was a song
Itself, and she was ravished. Sweet and low
She heard it—leaned and heard it, breathing so,
The very silence answered pure and strong.

How could he be uncertain? There she stood,
A fugitive this hour from those extremes—
Of fire in him, of ice—and called it good,
The difference. How can men throw gold away?
Yet it was not for me to think and say.
The mean of love is never what it seems.

My World's Body

"Identify the logs in the fireplace, burning?
They are not logs at all, if one remembers—
I do—where they lived, and made December's
Picture on blank snow; but the sun, returning,
Thickened the leaves above them, and discerning
Birds built in that darkness. These are members
Still of my world's body." "Even as embers?"
"Even as dust and ashes, even as learning—"

"Oh! Don't say it. Death?" "Why not, my dear?
This blaze came suddenly, by our own act,
But they know now." "Don't say it!" "Then you fear
Before your time. Have we been carried in?
Has any match been lighted? And a thin
Smoke started? Patience, dear, until the fact."

The Misanthrope

For he so loathed the world, this nameless man,
That he said nothing. Something was too much,
Was tribute, was a taste of him, a touch,
A wooing it to change. So as it ran
He watched it, like one pleased with any plan
It had in its great head—that he would clutch
And crush could this be secret, and not such
A glory as never was since time began.

The world, unguessing, went upon its way
Toward its own end, that no one still has seen.
On his deep grave the shadows fall as green
As anywhere since hate and love were born;
Since noiseless night, since musical noonday;
And death down under, fingering his horn.

Remembered Gaiety

Remembered gaiety hurts mind and heart
As present pain is impotent to do.
The moment's loss, courageously lived through,
Can die; but not those sudden days that start
And breathe again, immortally apart
From earlier, from after. They are few,
And chance's children; yet their smiles renew
More sadness than death does with all his art.

The people in this picture think to stand
On this same rock forever; he that waves,
And she that simpers—underneath what sun
Do they lie now, forgetting? Wind and sand
That blow here since— O, tell me why time saves,
Merciless, one moment, only one?

Who We Are

It never is ourselves that we hear talking.
Just under, or way over—thus it blows,
That wind of words, and not a listener knows
Of the small animal between sleepwalking,
Who slips from sight and sound, and from all stalking
Strangers. Down and down their circles close,
Then hover nothing; they are cuckoos, crows,
And jackdaws to this dove they would be hawking.

Or so we tell ourselves, not speaking plain,
Not honoring Time the hunter. Late or soon
He finds us; piece by piece, and heart by brain,
He picks us out of darkness. Who we are
We say at last, like any stone or star,
Or fellow man, or face of the full moon.

If Luck Has Senses

If luck has senses and perceives us here,
And punishes our boasting, is it eyes—
Sharp lidded, laughing, since we think us wise?—
Or feelers in the dark that bring her near,
Then break us? Or a single ass's ear,
Suspicious? Or a sting to paralyze
This pride in us that vainly, vainly tries
The very edge of danger falling sheer?

For something in her knows. We tap the wood,
We tell her not to come, yet even now
She listens. Or she looks. Or the thin hood
That hides her trembles quick, as if with breath.
Or is she woman? Short of sudden death,
Luck will not answer who, or when, or how.

Nature's Grace

So natural his grace, men called it more.
They said it was God's own, descended thus
On this light walker who so dazzled us,
Sometimes, we turned away and shut the door.
Yet never sharply. Envy was not sore,
Beholding him, nor were they perilous,
Those eyes, so inward fair, so courteous,
We dreamed of angel times gone long before.

These were the latter days, when men forgot
How spendthrift nature is. With empty space
She plays, rebuilding heaven and old hell
Most cunningly, most like. Yet not so well
That her own maker is deceived; yet not
So wisely that he names it his, the grace.

None But Death

How was it when he knew that none but Death
Had come for none but him? He of all men,
He must have been the most unready. Then,
There was this stranger. Oh, it takes our breath,
Thinking of his that stopped. The preacher saith,
Prepare. But how was he to die again
Who never once had dreamed it—even when
This burden grew that every man downlayeth?

He bore the dark sky lightly. He looked out
As if from under happy leaves, in showers.
But a wild storm—he carried that about
Daylong upon his head; nor laughed at those
Like us who could not. Now the beaten rose
Lies flat. The heavens fell. Weep, all you flowers.

Equal to Equal

Courtesy was born among the stars.
They were the first to sing as love looked down
On morning's chaos, heaving. Still the frown
Of fear on every face, and rumored wars
Of thunder between worlds. So love in tears
Sat looking. But creation did not drown
Like death in its own silence—oh, that sound
At silver sunrise, east among the stars.

Nor were the dark ones modest. Great and small,
They sang alike, each one of them more proud
For knowing each was master, and could call,
Equal to equal, across heaven's waste.
And yet it was no desert if they faced
Due inwardly and smiled, and sometimes bowed.

Cold Change

Nothing is more implacable than change—
Cold change, the heart's hard enemy—except
His will that one time made it. Then he slept.
And sleeping still, beyond the farthest range
Of fashion, there he lies, and is more strange
Even than time that breaks us. He has kept
No tally of our losses, nor has wept
At the worst woes our folly could arrange.

For we ourselves play doom, and dare the years
Never to alter. Or we think and shift
As if we too were gods, and turn the gears
Of the great engine that he built; and lift
Our fortunes—oh, a little. But our fears
Fall with us, in eternity's downdrift.

What Beast Is This?

What beast is this, not bellowing, not stung
With blood, that moves upon us to devour?
For it is near—the never ending hour
Of our own death, that all the saints have sung.
But where is the great animal? Among
What rushes does he build his ruinous bower?
Why is he not louder? So much power,
And hidden! All that fury, and no tongue!

Be still. How do you know the beast is strange?
Look in your neighbor's eyes. He may be there.
Look in your own. Nothing so much can change
As man. The very foulest was most fair
In Eden. Then be still and let him range,
That shadow monster met upon the stair.

Humanity Unlimited

Humanity unlimited? Oh, ring
Fire bells; unleash the bloodhounds, and the tall
Mastiffs; and start building, somewhere, wall
On wall that daws and eagles on the wing
But no proud man can pass. Do anything,
My masters, to confine us one and all—
You, too—within the pasture and the hall
And the gray church where sadness used to sing.

It sang that we were prisoners of ourselves,
And jailers—oh, the echo doubled back
And crushed us. There was not a lighted crack
That let the worst, the best of us go through.
Yet it was sweeter. Mice upon the shelves
Of our great cupboard envied us; and you.

Yes, I Know

Political our life is—yes, I know.
The common good is golden, and the deed
Most manly is to love it, and to lead
Those other ones that hesitate to go—
Look at them. Their souls are pale as snow
With ignorance and fear. See how they feed
On darkness, and the root of such a weed
As wisdom might make blossom. Yes, I know.

Then why am I this season sunk so far
In my own shadow? Now am I the same
As others; nor do I remember still
That sun we saw together. Dangers are,
And deaths, and wide disasters. But my will—
Oh, woe—feeds on itself and stubborn shame.

The Time of Martyrs

The time of martyrs may be come again;
Yet as of old, no single heart is foul.
Security, blindfolded, wears the cowl;
Stupidity sits here and judges men.
The best are most despised, as they were then;
As long ago they did, the worst ones howl
Loudest of fair intentions—wolf and owl
And dark hyena, guarding our great den.

The time of martyrs may be come and gone,
And we too late discover what is lost.
The beaten dog most happily will fawn;
December's flower forgives October's frost.
The time of martyrs—is it aging on,
With no spring meadows waiting to be crossed?

The Deepest Dream

The deepest dream is of mad governors.
Down, down we feel it, till the very crust
Of the world cracks, and where there was no dust,
Atoms of ruin rise. Confusion stirs,
And fear; and all our thoughts—dark scavengers—
Feed on the center's refuse. Hope is thrust
Like wind away, and love sinks into lust
For merest safety, meanest of levelers.

And then we wake. Or do we? Sleep endures
More than the morning can, when shadows lie
Sharper than mountains, and the cleft is real
Between us and our kings. What sun assures
Our courage, and what evening by and by
Descends to rest us, and perhaps to heal?

The War God

The war god is not guilty any more.
Time was he winced, meeting our angry eyes.
And even then prevailed, yet knew it wise
Not to seem proud, sending sweet peace before
As sister, goddess, queen. But with a roar
Now he blasphemes her, and his bluster flies
Like desert wind, and fills the dirty skies.
He says that peace is his dishonest whore.

And who of us but laughs, though bitterly
We wonder at the change in us, and charge
Now him, now fate, with fathering such blood?
War's moment, lengthened to eternity—
What else is our religion? What so large,
So terrible? We worship it, the Flood.

Too Many Fears

God is not gone? Fear rules us as before?
But of too many things, the prophet said;
And counted them by tapping his lean head
Whose eyes so long had pondered, keeping score.
Those dreams that burrow nightly, and that bore
Still deeper all the day—as in the dark
Some worms, insatiable, are never fed—
Too many! And he sighed. But you have more.

Nor is one fear the father of the rest.
God is not gone? Then why are these so wild?
Why are they unnamed, why unconfessed?
Oh, none of them is dutiful, is child,
Is messenger to him whose terrible breast
Still broods; and still with mercy could be mild.

Again, That Laughter

Censorious, the old remember days
When punishment fell instantly on fools;
And knaves were not; or if they were, the rules,
Read to them on gallows, in the gaze
And audience of others, showed them ways
They should have gone. But now the ghosts and ghouls
Outnumber upright men, and mercy pules
Excuses at the center of its maze.

So croak the old ones, and the young ones smile
And say it is their weakness. Were they well,
And the blood bounded in them, they would pile
Pity on pity too, and take the shame
On their own shoulders. (Listen. There it came
Again, that laughter. Do they hear in hell?)

Born Brothers

Equality is absolute or no.
Nothing between can stand. We are the sons
Of the same sire, or madness breaks and runs
Through the rude world. Ridiculous our woe
If single pity does not love it. So
Our separate fathers love us. No man shuns
His poorest child's embrace. We are the sons
Of such, or ground and sky are soon to go.

Nor do born brothers judge, as good or ill,
Their being. Each consents and is the same,
Or suddenly sweet winds turn into flame
And floods are on us—fire, earth, water, air
All hideously parted, as his will
Withdraws, no longer fatherly and there.

The Prism

When Adam fell, and Eve, and the gates closed
Forever, with a clang that lightning now
Repeats, and thunder mourns, perfection dozed;
And dozes still, save that a happy brow
Sometimes in wind remembers, and somehow
Adam is not dead; the scarlet-rosed,
The green angelic garden he reposed
And climbed in sings again from every bough.

But all men since are gone. The patriarchs,
The heroes—even they were broken beams
Of the first morning light, that fell on larks
And lived—no single splinter of it lost,
As piecemeal in our minds the truth is tossed
On waves of darkness here, and dawn but seems.

There Was an Island

Did the gods ever, manifest in form,
Come to men's houses at the hour of meat,
And sit, and taste? And did small children greet
Their greatness, bringing coals to keep them warm?
They had come far, though instantly, through storm
And upper darkness. Did they rest their feet,
And did the housewife smile, and serve them sweet
Clear honey from the hive, the summer swarm?

There was an island, misty in the sea,
Where thus they wandered—not in stranger's guise,
Not beggarly, not human, but as he
Their chiefest lord once made them; and his eyes
Always were on them, lest they cease to be.
(Odysseus, tell us truly. Were they lies?)

And Now by Dark

The big and little stars that burn by night—
There is one time they should not, yet they do;
And all the more fiercely then, as if Great Who,
Great What so high above us loved this blight
Of dryness here, these streams sunk out of sight
And the green pastures withering—men, too,
And beasts, lamenting springs where coolness grew
By grace of thunderheads both black and white.

Now nothing but hot days and dying trees;
And now by dark, as we come out of doors,
These pitiless huge gazers—even these,
That once could hide, and did, in overcast
And whirlwind. But the time for that is past,
Old Scorpion sings, and licks his glittering sores.

After Long Drought

After long drought, commotion in the sky;
After dead silence, thunder. Then it comes,
The rain. It slashes leaves, and doubly drums
On tin and shingle; beats and bends awry
The flower heads; puddles dust, and with a sigh
Like love sinks into grasses, where it hums
As bees did once, among chrysanthemums
And asters when the summer thought to die.

The whole world dreamed of this, and has it now.
Nor was the waking easy. The dull root
Is jealous of its death; the sleepy brow
Smiles in its slumber; and a heart can fear
The very flood it longed for, roaring near.
The spirit best remembers being mute.

The People of the Word

And Did the Animals?

And did the animals in Noah's ark—
That was of oleander wood, with cabins
Cunningly bitumined in and out—
Did all those animals lie quietly?
For months and weeks and days, until the dove
Came home, and they were dry on Ararat,
Did every bird, with head beneath its wing,
Did every beast, with forepaws folded in,
Did every reptile, coiled upon itself,
Lie sleeping as no man did, patiently?
A man might think this tempest would not end,
Nor timbers cease to creak, nor the light come.
These did not know it rained, these did not know
Their kind survived in them if it survived.
A thinking man might doubt it, and in misery
Listen. Did they listen? But to what?
They did not know of time, they did not count
The waves. Then did they cry out in their dreams?
Or did they even dream, those specimen souls?

The Rainbow

"Though every man be evil in his mind
From the first breath of thought, I now do promise
Never again to wish all flesh destroyed,
Either by flood or fire." So Noah heard,
And wondered. Even the animals, God said,
Were safe beneath His rainbow—all poor things
With blood in them to come and go forever
As day and night did, and as winter, summer.
To live and die. Poor things, and yet His own.
So Noah wondered; and so all men since
Have said: Is it not strange, His disappointment?
For knowing all, He still knew not the deep ways
This creature most like Him was bound to go;
Or if not bound, did go, has gone, and will
Till the round earth itself no more is dreamed.
Is it not wonderful, men say, that even
He of the vast vision, even He
That brooded above the firmament, and fished
Each form out of the void, the desolation,
The darkness and the wind—oh, even He
Anticipated nothing. Not a soul,
They cry, but must amaze Him; so much more,
So other than His plan; all these recesses
Singing in the heart; all these volutions
Of the still motley serpent in the skull.
So all men since the rainbow, looking inward,
Have wondered at themselves; and flattered thus
The very flesh He wanted to destroy
Yet did not; for He pitied the poor thing.

The Prophet Enoch

Who were the sons of heaven that looked down
One day and saw earth's women and desired them?
Samyaza was their captain; Asael,
Urakabarameel, Yomyael,
Saraknyal, Zavebe, and Armers
Were prefects; all in all, two hundred angels
Fell that day so deep beyond redemption,
Only the darkest desert now contains
Their bones, that still are burning as they burned
That day they saw our women, and deployed
From Armon, wooing sweet flesh in the lowlands
Where men were, and their wives, and winsome
    daughters
Not meant for incorruptible delight.
In both it was corruption; neither earth
Nor heaven knew this thing until that day,
When curtained beds, and mosses in the fields,
And river banks and caverns by the ocean,
Shadowy with love, conceived in shame
A progeny of giants, who devoured
Earth's animals and fruits, and would have eaten
Man himself, had not the deluge come
That cleansed us. Angel to angel, dust to dust—
Love then was true once more, as still it is,
On earth as it is in heaven. For no woman,
Wife to a man, pollutes him. And no star,
Wed to another there, wanders mistaken.
Or so the prophet Enoch says and sings.

Abraham and Isaac

A solitary ram that day was grazing,
That day of all days, in Moriah grass.
Thin grass, and thoughtless ram. It did not need
To think, that silly sheep with the curled horns
Held ever downward, moving on and on
As if by its own choice—for instance now,
When it came near an old man with a knife
Uplifted. Shining knife, about to fall
On a stretched boy, silent among faggots.
Silent boy, eyes open, facing up.
All of Moriah, silent. The ram moved
Again—its ultimate free act, for brushwood
Caught the curled horns. It butted, but was caught.
And the old man listened. Not to this,
But listened. Then he looked, and his hand trembled,
Suddenly, with joy. The ram was here
By no thought of its own, nor was its last act
Free. It had been destined for this day,
And lived it as it should, head ever downward,
Moving on and on, even to where
This brushwood was, that rattled. But the old man,
Listening, had not heard so near a sound.
It was God's voice that said to him, Let be.
Only that soon he looked; and sacrificed,
Instead of his one lamb, this chosen sheep.

Rebekah

Abraham's old slave, come to the well
At Nahor, seeking water for his camels
And a good wife for Isaac, found Rebekah—
Perfect in simplicity, found one
Clear girl he could thank God for, and adorn
With rings and bracelets, and at sunrise take
Forever home to be the wife of Isaac.
Whom she deceived. Rebekah in her womb
Felt twins at war, and knew that she must favor
One above the other when both lived.
She favored Jacob; and if Isaac more
Loved Esau, with the hairy hands and neck
That smelled of dewy fields, and of wild animals
And grain, being her husband he was helpless.
For the same girl it was, grown old with him,
Who tricked him now by sending Jacob in
For the blind man's unalterable blessing.
The skin of kids betrayed him, so that Esau's
Sons, by Ishmael's daughter, and by ruder
Breeds, were never children of God's line.
But Jacob walked with angels, and his son
Was Joseph. So Rebekah the deceiver
Had the same mind that Abraham's old slave
Found once as clear as water. And it was.
Even that day she knew—or did she then?—
That she was God's own virgin, born at Nahor
To visit on these men this mortal hurt.
But guilty Jacob slept and dreamed of angels.

Dinah

For Dinah ravished, all of Shechem's city
Paid with all its blood. Shechem's, too,
Its chiefest prince, who longed for Dinah so—
To keep her, whom he ravished—he could smell
No craft in Dinah's brothers till they smote
And smote, and every house, red with the horror,
Died; even Shechem's, where in silence
Dinah sat. But her they rescued. And
She wept. Was it for joy? Or walking slow,
Did Dinah weep for justice—all the blood
Of all that lover's people drying now
In sunless rooms behind her? Did she turn
And look, and was it well that Shechem's face
No longer hoped for kindness in these eyes?
For afterward-consent? Shechem's hands—
Did Dinah shudder? Nothing tells of this,
Or anything she thought that bloody day
Her brothers bore her home, and she could hear
The captive herds about her—all the sheep,
Bewildered, and the beaten asses braying.

Joseph Wept

"The old man of whom you spoke—your father—
Is he yet living? Is he well?" Red-eyed,
The sons of Leah nodded. "And your youngest
Brother, of whom you told me—is this he?"
For Benjamin stood there, clear-lidded, beautiful,
The son of his own mother Rachel. And four more,
That maids had bred. But Benjamin alone
Was cause that Joseph went into his room
And shut the door and wept. The twelve of them—
All here, with Jacob far away in Canaan,
Starving. All together at this end
Of bitter time. For ten of them had hated
Joseph, their bright brother. Only Benjamin,
Whose blessed birth had been the death of Rachel,
Only he had not. Therefore these tears.
And yet the ten that sold him into Egypt,
The ten his dreams offended—they were cause,
And older. For he thought: I was the bright one;
I dreamed and told my dreams. I did not hide
My light in loving clouds; I did not shame
To shine full in their faces. Was it God's
Cunning and deep purpose so to cleave us
That now and here, in Egypt, a thin remnant
Of Israel might live? Nevertheless
I boasted, and despised them; thought me different,
And better. And I was. But am no more.
The dozen is made one. God's miracle
Is that we all are met—they in their garments,
Bowing, and I in mine, a gorgeous stranger,
Lofty, and their lord. Now I must go,

Must speak to them: "I am your brother Joseph;
Our father—is he well?" Then all shall weep—
I know it. Can I do this? Can I still
Not weep myself? Yet why should I not weep?
Why should there be that difference then, when none
Is here now in my heart? So half in fear
He bathed his face and opened the gold door
Between them, and sat down with them to eat.

Joseph and Jacob

In a swift chariot, with horses jingling
The red gold of their bridle ornaments,
Joseph drove deep into the land of Goshen,
Then stopped. This might be Jacob, his old father,
Coming. And it was. The patient wagons,
The sheep, the cattle, herded by good hands,
The asses' pointed ears, and all those people—
Fifty, sixty, seventy—it was Israel
Coming. And he walked ahead to meet them,
Looking right and left for the old man
His father, who had thought him dead. "My son!
Now that I have seen you, I can die."
Here then he was, descended from the forward
Wagon. And he limped. Come all the way
From Canaan, in the desert dust, he limped—
A small old man, the socket of whose thigh
Still hurt him. And they fell upon each other,
Weeping: Joseph, vice-king of all Egypt,
In linen robes, with gold about his neck
And a great signet ring, and sons at home
By Asenath, the daughter of the priest
Of On, by whom he almost had forgotten
Israel and its woes—Joseph mingled
His tears with those of Jacob, who one night,
So long ago that only a hip remembered,
Wrestled in the dark with God's tall angel,
And won. But when the day broke over Penuel,
He limped; and ever had while Joseph dreamed
In Egypt, that rich dying land, and prospered
By famine. Now from Canaan these had come,

These many sons of Jacob, with their wives
And children. Sixty-six, the whole of Israel,
Exiled. They were desolate and poor,
But young; and they would multiply; and Joseph,
Savior of them all, would be forgotten.
Brilliant in his linen and his gold,
And welcoming their caravan with tears
And smiles, even he would be forgotten.
For he was not of them, this prince of Nile
Whom God Himself one day would scarce remember.

How Moses Saw God

"No man can look upon my face and live.
My glory you may see, but not myself."
The people at the bottom of the mountain,
Nor Aaron, nor the elders, heard Jehovah
Say it, topmost there on Sinai,
Beyond the cloud whose darkness hid the truth
As thunder hatches lightning. And already
Trumpets had sounded, and already fire,
Seeming to consume itself, had smoldered,
Smoldered, then had vanished. But the mind
Of Moses heard, and his ears trembled. "Man—
I know your name—retire into that cleft
Of rock while this my glory passes by.
My hand will hold you there. Be not afraid.
It shall be more impossible to look
Than, having looked, to live. Be not afraid."
So He that was no other than He was
Passed by, and did not turn again. And Moses,
Gazing as into sunset, saw God's back;
And bowed; and fasted all of forty days
And forty nights in wonder; then went down
To his own people, waiting. Who in fear
Avoided him. For now his very skin,
As if it had been tested in a furnace,
Glowed; and they avoided him, until
He veiled himself. As thunder wraps hot lightning,
So Moses hid the truth of what he saw
On Sinai that day. No other man
Has seen as much; and even he but saw
God's back, as at the setting of all suns
That ever yet have risen or will rise.

Jephthah's Daughter

Jephthah, son of a harlot, had one daughter,
Born in the land of Tob, where he with brigands
Raided the flocks and herds. But Gilead's sons,
His brothers, who had banished him, were sorry,
And sent for him to come and save them now.
"And if the Ammonites go down before me,
Then will I be your chief?" They swore it, Yes,
And armed him; and he vowed, if he were victor,
That the first living creature whom at Mizpeh
He met by his own door should die for God.
He triumphed, and rode home; and lo, this daughter
Ran to him—with tambourines and dancing
Ran to him; and wondered why he wept,
And why he tore his clothes. "My only child"—
So then she knew, and knelt. But when no blow
Descended—none was ready, in his weakness—
She cried to him: "For two months let me live.
Alone among the mountains let me wander
With my few maidens, mourning my estate."
For not one man had known her, and no man
But Jephthah would be desolate that day,
Two full moons hence, when the keen knife must fall.
If he consented gladly, did he rest then?
Did Jephthah rest? The thing was still to do.
A thousand hours, each one of them more terrible
Than this one that was over—yet not over—
How could he pass them? How did Jephthah, chieftain,
Son of a harlot, pass them? No one hears;
Or whether on the mountains she regretted,
Too, that gift of time—all those sunrises,

Powerless to prepare her for the dark arms
Of the one husband she would have at last;
And had at last; and lies with him eternally,
Mourning her bright maidenhood below.

The Ark of the Covenant

An empty box, the sons of Baal said;
Nothing inside except the mumbling words
Of one no man remembered; he had lived
On mountains long ago, and he had lighted
Israel out of Egypt; but where now,
And who, and why should any stout foe fear him?
So they abducted the acacia chest
That Moses built and overlaid with gold
Inside and out; even the rings and poles
He overlaid with gold; and placed inside it
Nothing but parchment texts of the decrees
He heard on Sinai once, and well remembered.
Nothing but those. Yet bloody death was in them
For the stout sons of Baal: plagues and tempests,
And Dagon falling down, and slaughtered thousands
Crying upon the silence; for no sword
But silence, silence killed them. So the Philistines,
Secretly, by night, sent home the terrible
Box; and the bearers listened; but no sound
Came out of it, no mumbling. It was the silence,
Silence, that had killed them. "Thou shalt have
No other gods before me." Even this
No bearer heard; for the deep sleep of faith
Was on the world that night; and if a dream
Disturbed it, Israel too shook in her bed,
Foreseeing all the shame, all the forgetting.

Last of the Judges

"Then you may have your king." And the proud people
Shouted. But they had not listened close.
They had not heard the whirlwind in his throat,
Whispering God's wrath; for now as always,
Samuel, their pure judge, was but a horn
Through which the past and future blew, and truth,
Welcome or unwelcome, hummed in the airways.
It hummed there now, and doomed them, but they
    laughed
And shouted. Even now, his head and shoulders
Higher than the highest, Saul was wandering
In search of lost she-asses; and became
Their king; and blundered daily; till his death
Was their death too, though David's time, succeeding,
And Solomon's, seemed blissful. But it blew,
That whirlwind, even then, and only struck
As the long sun of Israel went down
On Jeroboam raging, and the white bones
Of Jezebel, that no wild dog would eat,
Manuring the dead fields that still would mourn,
In utter darkness, hideous captivity,
While prophets groaned, and some few souls remembered
How the proud people once had wanted kings;
Thrice warned, had wanted kings; and here they had
    them;
And the hoarse words of Samuel, and the lost love
Of God were but as desert lamentations
In a cold corner of the night as far
Away and long ago as Abraham.

Michal

Michal, that she-wife whom David had
For his first comforter, from Saul her father—
But then in fury Saul withdrew the gift—
Michal was another man's awhile;
Was Paltiel's; till David, king himself,
Remembered, and he sent for her by Abner.
Instantly she started—with what words
And what good-bys to Paltiel we know not,
Or whether with embraces. Yet we know
This husband followed, weeping all the way
And watching—all the bleak way to Bahurim
Watching David's wife who was his own,
His own. And yet no longer. So the dust
Was bitter that he breathed; till at Bahurim
Abner, looking down, said "Go, return";
And Paltiel returned. But Michal went
Straight on, the bitter wind sweet in her nostrils,
To where the king was whom another day,
When both of them were older, she would scorn
For dancing in an apron, by the ark
Of God. And he would hate her till she died.
And she would bear no children, either his
Or Paltiel's, until she groaned and died.

Abigail

She met him in a wild pass of the mountains—
David, whom she called her lord, and said:
"I bring you bread and wine, I bring you raisins.
Sheep I bring, and corn, and cakes of figs.
Accept all these, my lord; I am your servant;
I save you from blood-guilt. For you are bound
Where Nabal is, my husband, who insulted
Certain of your soldiers. Do not kill him.
Nabal's very name, my lord, is Fool.
Then do not kill him. When my lord is king,
What pity if a fool's blood blights his conscience.
I am your servant, saving you." He looked,
Beautiful himself, upon her beauty,
And said: "So shall it be. Blessed are you
That kept me from revenge. I would have killed him,
Surely. Go in peace." And David left her.
Then was it with his beauty in her heart
That she went straight to Nabal, who was drunk,
And told him of the danger there had been,
So that his spirit sank in him, like stone,
And in ten days he died? For she was ready
At Carmel when those messengers came in
With word that David wanted her for wife.
She mounted up at once and rode to him,
And married him forever, and forgot—
Or did you, Abigail, that first one's fall?

Bathsheba

When Bathsheba, grown old, one day had audience
With David who was dying—she must speak
For Solomon, their son, against the danger
Of Adonijah's coming to be king—
Abishag was there. But Bathsheba
Looked elsewhere; only warned of Adonijah,
Then went as she had come. Did she remember,
Did Bathsheba remember, worlds ago,
Being Uriah's wife whom David saw
On the hot roof, in sun and shadow bathing?
The shadows were against the one great eye
That burned there, and the little ones of men—
On which reflecting, she grew warm with shame;
And turned; and someone told her David saw.
The great eye now was his; the sun went out
In worlds of heat that builded unto heaven—
Save that it was not heaven. For Uriah
Died in war, by David's word, and God
Was not well pleased. And yet they lived,
Those lovers; were the king, the queen; and Solomon
Lived next, whom Adonijah on this day
Threatened to unthrone. So Bathsheba
Spoke only of their son; not of the beautiful
Abishag who stood beside the bed,
And every night lay in it, on the bosom
Of the cold king, whom fleeces could not comfort,
Nor silks, nor the far fire. Only this maiden,
Beautiful as blood, sustained his heart
As once Uriah's wife did, worlds away
And wars ago. So David listened, shivering,

Till Bathsheba retired, and dark came down,
And Abishag lay curled inside his long cloak
Like a warm worm in leaves. While Bathsheba,
Alone, with no eye on her, God's or man's,
Sat wondering at this moonlight in the room,
And yet no moon. Was it his mind, remembering,
And following, and feeling her poor warmth?

Sarah of Ecbatana

Tobias, son of Tobit, felt desire
For Sarah, the sad daughter of Raguel,
Before he ever saw her. Could this be?
She was of his people, far away,
And destined for him, Azariah said;
And beautiful, and sensible; but sad
Because of seven bridegrooms she had lost
On seven wedding nights—a demon's work,
Not hers, although the maids accused her so.
The angel Azariah said: "Go up
To her, Tobias, and possess her without fear;
For she is yours, and was from the beginning;
Pray with her, then draw the curtains close,
And sleep all night; I tell you it is well."
And so Tobias, with obedient heart,
Was full of love for Sarah long before
He ever saw Ecbatana, her city.
She was of his people; and was beautiful,
And sensible; and wanted to be dead
Because she did not know the very boy
Was coming who could save her, and whose bride
In truth, not lust, she was from the beginning.
So Azariah said, whose other name
Was Raphael; and obedient Tobias
Eagerly walked with him all the way.

The Word

The people whom He chose to hear His word
Had the one mind that could remember it.
And with what heat they did, until captivity
Cooled them. Or it seemed to. For their voice,
Grown inward now, repeated not to deserts
Nor the wind ears of aliens what they knew
Of further things unfolded, of the hidden
Person who was coming—always coming,
And they alone knew why. Yet knew not when.
For the one people He could trust with truth
Had then this terrible, this inward duty
Forever to deny it. He must fail
Who came. Or seem to fail. Oh, the dark word
That in their long captivity they warmed,
Lest truth itself grow cold and die—oh, word,
Oh, wonder, it is still by their surviving
Saved; and by their silence, that keeps warm
And dark the word that too much sun would kill.

Soul and Circumstance

Praise Him, Praise Her

Praise him, praise her, praise all
Soft steppers, all slow smilers,
All sweet sleepers under
The stars. For they praise them.

By foot, by face, by lying
In bed so lightly, these
Praise them, and therefore Him:
He made them sing together.

And still He does; they know it;
They listen, and they move
Like dancers, and all night
They smile in their sweet sleep.

So far it is down hither—
Praise them, His poor children
Who think they do so little
For this immense reward.

Praise Doubt

Praise the good angel doubt,
Guardian of us that walk
On the deep waters of this world.

Praise him. He never rests,
However weary the way
Over these dark, salt, dangerous meadows.

Do not look down, he says;
Beware with me and the sun
Of faith's innumerable caverns.

Monsters can be there.
You will have plenty of time.
Too soon descending, you are devoured.

Praise him. He believes
In the long day we are given.
Praise him. He dances upon the whitecaps.

Never Another

Praise Him who makes us happy
When not another would;
There is so little reason
In our so little good.

Praise Him who waits all morning,
All afternoon, all night,
All year until this moment
Of that arriving light;

Praise Him who sends it dancing,
Praise Him who lets us see,
And move with it, and listen,
And sing, soberly.

Praise Him who when we lose it,
And twilight thickens sound,
Remembers where we slumber;
Marks this nether ground;

And waits upon our waking
As never another would;
Praise Him who is the reason,
Praise Him, the only good.

The God of Galaxies

The god of galaxies has more to govern
Than the first men imagined, when one mountain
Trumpeted his anger, and one rainbow,
Red in the east, restored them to his love.
One earth it was, with big and lesser torches,
And stars by night for candles. And he spoke
To single persons, sitting in their tents.

Now streams of worlds, now powdery great whirlwinds
Of universes far enough away
To seem but fog-wisps in a bank of night
So measureless the mind can sicken, trying—
Now seas of darkness, shoreless, on and on
Encircled by themselves, yet washing farther
Than the last triple sun, revolving, shows.

The god of galaxies—how shall we praise him?
For so we must, or wither. Yet what word
Of words? And where to send it, on which night
Of winter stars, of summer, or by autumn
In the first evening of the Pleiades?
The god of galaxies, of burning gases,
May have forgotten Leo and the Bull.

But God remembers, and is everywhere.
He even is the void, where nothing shines.
He is the absence of his own reflection
In the deep gulf; he is the dusky cinder
Of pure fire in its prime; he is the place
Prepared for hugest planets: black idea,
Brooding between fierce poles he keeps apart.

Those altitudes and oceans, though, with islands
Drifting, blown immense as by a wind,
And yet no wind; and not one blazing coast
Where thought could live, could listen—oh, what word
Of words? Let us consider it in terror,
And say it without voice. Praise universes
Numberless. Praise all of them. Praise Him.

Dialogue in December

In so much dark no light is little.
    But can light be at the end of the year?
Only listen. It will come.
    And put out dying? And put out fear?
Yes, but listen. Good heart, listen.
    I do, I do—I see, I hear.

That star is enough in this much night.
    It glitters. But a child has cried.
He is the first one in the world.
    Even the old world, that died?
Even the new—he is all the living.
    And all the dead—are they satisfied?

Listen and look. Is there any weeping?
    Only for comfort, only for joy.
Only for love. But the child that was crying—
    He is a beautiful, strange boy.
He is little and weak, this lord of the world.
    But oh, too strong, too strong to destroy.

What We Wanted

Good old rain god, somewhere now
He sits and sends it, what we wanted.
He was dozing, with his hat off,
But it drips again and soaks him;
Droops around him, beard and shoulder;
Hangs there heavy, like his greatcoat,
All the skirts of which run rivers.

Good old sender, there he sits
Supposing this is all we wanted.
And it is, upon the shingles,
And it is, among the hay roots;
Not a horny tree but thanks him.
So he blinks and is complacent:
He has wetted all his children.

Good old ancient, doze again.
There was something else we wanted.
There is still this desert inward,
These hot thorns that hurt each other.
You have nothing for that ailment,
It was not in the beginning,
There is no way rain can reach it.

Good old giver, nevertheless,
Thank you, thank you. It was wanted.
We receive it as the daisies,
We declare it with the puddles—
Listen, listen, on the windows!
Long enough, and who remembers?
Yet we do. It is our weakness.

The Six Swans of Grimm

Their tongue-bound sister, terrified,
Thought only of the starting flame—
Not yet; the faggots were still cold;
But round her now a crackling came—
Not really; it was in her mind,
With panic and supposéd shame.

And yet the king, and yet the crowd,
Heard something too, and looked aloft.
A wedge of wings it was that made
This roaring in the air so soft,
This whirr, as pure white feathers fell
On tower and mead and fence and croft.

"My brothers!" For the six were there,
Standing in coats that proved them men.
"My brothers!" But they did not know
How wonderful it was again
For the sweet words to fly away
Like wind and smoke, like raven and wren.

Soul and Circumstance

Wait not, my soul, on circumstance;
It does not wait for you.
It nibbles at you now, and will
Devour you; I say true.

For I have seen its hungry face
Be satisfied with one
That stood like you, uncertain here,
Thinking himself alone.

And so he was; but circumstance
Was not the friend he lacked.
He had not yet the bitter taste
And strength of his own act.

Insipid sweet, he still denied
Himself and his great kind.
And so I saw him eaten through
And spit away like rind.

The Problem of Good

Ponder as you may, philosopher,
This excellent spirit,
You will not reach the origin
Of so much merit.
The white secret rose
Blooms without cause;
And dying, leaves nothing here for mind to inherit.

The black one, if you will, sir,
Connect with coal;
The red one with river clay;
The brown with wool.
Imperfection sits
Impatiently, and waits
To see itself in intellect, that loves it after all.

Stare into it long, philosopher,
This blinding goodness.
There will be no reflection in it
Of your rudeness.
The white, white rose
Is older than its cause,
Like the great sun, that never thinks upon its gladness.

Nothing Returns

Evil abominates the good
Because the good does not explain.
There was no reason Ruth could give
Except to speak her love again;
And then to prove it with a deed
As soon as Naomi had need.

Cold Iago, though, went mad,
Seeing simplicity in power;
Judas could not bear at last
Perfection's music hour by hour;
And struck, but with a senseless kiss
That made the very god we miss.

Evil is sooner understood,
Yet not for this, that still is strange:
It looks upon its opposite
And hates it without hope of change;
Evil abominates and burns;
But all is waste. Nothing returns.

Beauty Is

Beauty is not had,
Beauty is not made.
Beauty hates narrow;
Is wind-wide.

Beauty is not studied,
Beauty is not sold.
Beauty is no king's,
No church's child.

Beauty is not delicate,
Beauty is not dear.
Beauty will break out
Anywhere.

Anywhere beauty is,
All men smile;
Except its prophets;
And they fall.

The Good Workman

From there to here, from then till now—
What patience brought him all the way?
What knowing how to wait? And yet
He was not idle any day.

Each thing he did was done for best,
But then tomorrow, glancing down,
He shook his head; and with our smiles
Mingled his own secret frown.

Not that the way was endless; here,
Master of all but death, he lies.
The wonder is the patience—how
He lived with time, and took each rise

As water does, that waits for waves
However close it feels the shore;
As love does, that considers long:
Most is last, and child of more.

To Him That Hath

Those are helped who need no help.
To him that hath it shall be given.
So we see it is on earth,
And so we hear it is in heaven.

And is it true for saints as well:
To them that know it shall be told?
He that was loved is loved again?
He that was lonely—still cold?

And is it terrible at last?
"What else?" the falling pebble sings.
"What juster than this gravity,
That saves me all that waste of wings?

"What mercy is it would permit
My wandering away from here?
From there"—and into center sank
As morning meteors disappear.

If They Spoke

The animals will never know;
Could not find out; would scarcely care
That all their names are in our books,
And all their images drawn bare.

What names? They have not heard the sound,
Nor in their silence thought the thing.
They are not notified they live;
Nor ask who set them wandering.

Simply they are. And so with us;
And they would say it if they spoke;
And we might listen; and the world
Be uncreated at one stroke.

The Animals Slept On

The answer came by dream.
"They do not know of death.
So they can sleep and sleep,
And never count their breath;
They do not live by number,
The very name of death."

The animals slept on.
They did not know I heard.
"And therefore every conscience
Of every beast and bird
Is free as air, as water,
Of what the wind has heard."

The animals lay still;
They did not know I dreamed;
And let the world turn with them
Entirely as it seemed;
And sleeping was but waking,
And waking was but dreamed.

When the World Ends

The Mirror

Nothing could this man dismay.
He held a mirror in his hand:
A small one, but it looked away
As time does over sleeping land.

It showed him worse things coming yet;
So all our present, by compare,
Was only bitter, was Tibet,
To those ice absolutes of air.

He saw the poles beyond whose white
Two tireless eyes gazed here at him;
And had been gazing since the night
Before creation's interim;

And still would gaze when time again
Slept in eternity's slow arms;
That hushed the seas, and muffled men
Against great waves and wars' alarms.

Yet no man now. Each is his own.
He smiled; he pocketed the glass.
Serenity in him alone
Lives on and on, alas, alas.

Breathing Was Hard Enough

Breathing was hard enough,
Poor body,
With my child mind that altered hour by hour,
Startled by mouse fears, dreaming
Intimately, self-pleased,
Of ghosts that did not matter.

Breathing was harder still,
Tough body,
But you did not complain when gathering storms
Struck at us both, and proved,
Palpably, in man's day,
My terror was full grown.

Breathe in and out with me
Now, body—
Now—breathe in and out, as by a machine
Built to keep two alive—
It may, those doctors tell us—
Oh, in this worst of worlds.

Breathe on as if the best,
Tired body,
But waited, for the time of man is long;
But waited, like the deathless
Air, and like my mind,
That will survive this song.

The Same Stones

The same stones, one upon the other, stand.
Walls, familiar, do not fall.
The people, going, never cease to go.
There is no body-change at all.

No liquefaction. Yet what deadly eye,
Cold as the future, and as thin,
Has been here, looking? Not a thing but shows
Where one of those sharp rays went in.

Shot through, the inaccessible
Center is no longer dark, no longer
Soft, concealing
Firm seed, secret of the form to come:
Familiar form, like its own father's once,
Yet singular, yet strange;
Yet looked for, and—delivered—oh,
Most loved.
The arrows of what deadly cold,
What needle gazer,
Through and through have pierced it? What
Distinction now of out, of in?
All, all translucent—oh, this universe of glass
The keen ray threaded and exposed at heart:
All breakable,
All brittle,
All ready for the last
Change coming—when?

The same stones, one above the other, rest.
The people still stream up and down.
No alteration in the wind and rain.
No prophecy that earth will drown.

No image melting. Yet what thinnest god
Lives in the crevices and laughs?
Thief in the vein—what principle exults,
Dreaming of deep things' epitaphs?

That woman there, that man,
That dozing doorway, and that cobbled street,
That flagpole—none suspects,
Yet each of them already
Changes; each
Is riddled by a million splinter lines
Of chill light inward. Glass,
All glass.
The ancient shape without the ancient center—
Nothing will go but that.
And that—already
It is gone, with its soft seed
Of darkness, its firm secret
Of the surprising, the familiar form
That ever, ever was to come
And now will not come,
Ever.
It lies there still but is transfixed, is air;
Hides, visible,
As water does in water,
Ice in ice.

The same stones, next to one another, sleep.
Nothing is different by day.
Nightly the same men listen to this wind.
Every substantial thing will stay.

Will last its while, but with what missing part,
What core that crystal death preserves?
Already frost is white upon the vein;
And shines among the inmost nerves.

The World Waits

The world waits, holding its breath so quietly,
Death's rattle sounds like prophet's bones.
No desert raven ever was so raucous;
No other end threatened so many thrones.

Of big and little kings, of poor maids' men,
Of farmers in the field, of mice in burrow—
No sovereignty now, no subject sand;
No world, for there will be no more tomorrow.

So possibility, with half its voice,
Suspends the whole of this most panic time.
The held breath hears nothing but the croak
Of glories that were proper in our prime.

The song nobody sings—what did it say?
Goodness is difficult, and yet can be?
Death is certain? But the terrible raven
Says that, says that, too, unstoppably.

Was there no different thing bright angels knew?
Still was it thus when gods walked here as men?
Always the world has waited? O, white bird
Of morning, tell the dark truth more sweetly then.

Orion: October

As firelogs hiss, Orion gleams
Recumbent in the eastern cold;
And did when not a roof was here,
Nor any brain to think him old.

We go outdoors in fall and stare
At each of his great seven stars,
And number all the sunken ships
It witnessed, all the risen wars.

But he was there when not an eye
Looked into his, when not an earth.
No direction yet was named
When that deep universe had birth.

Nor cold nor hot. How white he is,
How ancienter than frost or fire.
We go back in. We shut him out.
Oblivion's sons forget the sire.

How Deep to Go

How deep to go, how dark,
O you that made all things in number,
How deep, how dark shall my desire descend?
And is there any happy coming
Home from that cold end?

There have been those that dived,
O you that made all things in weight,
Until solidity, that locks things in,
Suspending mind and body both—
Where did that death begin?

Why should it not be good,
O you that made all things in measure,
Not to sink deeper than the nether side
Of this we see, this film of world
Spread now so fine, so wide?

How near, and yet how changed,
O you whose glass stands always full,
How bright might this reality then be,
By undermirror watched; how warm,
And how quicksilver free.

Soon and Soon

As through the unthinking body waves of wellness
Once more run (mysterious their start;
Where was it? What the spring whose agitation,
Gentle at first, then overwhelmed the heart?
Then sent these racing outward: little seas
That break in joy at blood's extremities?);

As happiness, that thinks not but is thought,
Returns and tells us we are sound again,
So that we can forget, as spirit does,
The channels of permission; thus—yet when,
Yet where and why?—the sick world on some day
Will mend and smile, and put its self away;

Will neither feel its body nor its mind,
Nor the deep cause to which the soul consents;
Nor, intricate, the history; for oblivion,
Here at last, still hushes all events.
So, in the world's great nature, be it now.
Or soon and soon. (Say not a word of how.)

When the World Ends

When the world ends it is too much to hope,
And yet I do, that neither knife nor rope,
Nor sudden flame, nor worse than sudden freeze,
Is executioner. No less than these
Implacable, what if gold autumn came
And stayed till it was weary—spread the same
Cool hectic over waters and wild boughs
That now arrives for but a week's carouse;
Then winter? What if such a wonder fall
Kept on as if it were the end, the all?
What if it were, and centuries of red
So flushed each field and roof and river bed
That death itself lay down, and nothing died
Till all things did, beneath a shower as wide
As oceans of together-dropping leaves?
What if it were, and still no late reprieves
Canceled the utter end? I do not keep
That hope; and yet I dream of this slow sleep,
This indolent, this all but evermore
October such as never came before.

Death Went Away

Death Went Away

The little fox, demanding to be seen
In the cut field that fall, was not so little
To the first eyes he found, the middle-old ones,
The still ones over the wall, that saw in secret
Faraway death—huge death, the silent sender
Of neat four-footed omens saying Now,
Or pretty soon, make ready; this is the last
Surprise; nothing more comes out of the woods
In your time, ailing fellow. So they stared,
Those eyes, as every day the cricket hunter—
Or was it mice he pounced on—paused and looked;
Rippled his tail and pounced; then looked again.
He wanted to be seen. He came for that.
Quizzical, he pricked his ears and waited
On the smooth rise, and smiled his tapering smile—
All wizened fates in one, triangular—
That said: Come on, the dark long since was ready.
He did this every day that rainless fall.
And if the boy there, and the girl, clapped hands,
And the full-skirted wife ran twice to watch,
It was not thus at all for the tired father
Who turned and counted, then was off again
To the bleak woods, to the big hemlock clearing
Where the arms hung that cracked the useless bones,
That put the last light out.
                              But the light, living,
Put the omen out. So he remembers,
Smilingly, this man, and sees in secret
Faraway foxes, well in their winter holes.

Midway the Race

Black time that blinds me—
Steals my peace—
Oh, could we stop
Midway the race.
But while I sigh,
He simply is.

And yet no end
Save night on night.
I know this well—
Oh, could I wait,
Oh, could I watch,
Remembering that.

Oh, to stand still,
With him the thief
So manacled
That I might laugh,
Then push him down,
Cliff after cliff,

Till, feather-falling
And wing-light,
We floated both
In the immense white,
In the vast Now
(Not yet, not yet).

As Time Makes Love

One quick breath, and home resumes.
One wide eye, then staring stops.
The traveller, caressed and fed,
Is no more new than time that drops,
That drops here as it always did,
Like love, on his own coffin lid.

Where has he been? What siren sang?
They ask it, but their ears are sealed.
Already they are listening,
As if far off, to honey spilled,
Drop after drop. Slow and alone,
Familiar love makes monotone.

And would forever, save that sweets
Can tire of dropping in one place.
All these must wither, as he must,
And lie with stone across the face;
Never listening again
As time makes love to other men.

Memorandum

Things on my desk to be remembered.
Tomorrow, and next Monday. Next May.
Next world, almost. Yet certainly
Not that. No need of letters to myself
About not being here. Not yet.

I do remember, though, some friends
Who now are nowhere. And their pages, blown
By an illiterate wind, nobody
Reads. They certainly do not. They come,
They go, regardless, disengaged.

And I remember the tall marble
One of them is named on. Who was that?
I hear the passing question. Why
Was he? The youngest asker will be gone
When any echo wanders back.

So I have written this white slip.
Where shall I put it? Bottommost, perhaps.
Topmost, though, is better still.
It notifies the looker, and the smooth wood
He leans on: both of you, remember.

Time Didn't Love Me

Was the hound lonely that you and I saw there,
Trotting in the dusk? Do you think he was?
Where he had been, and whither he was going,
Neither of us knew, and I laughed; it is strange—
He did not hear me, and so I remember:
A long while ago, but I see him in the great field,
Trotting toward the river and those ancient trees.
Every night he did this? Probably, for water.
But that isn't it. He was serious, I say.
Like the last man on earth, he was serious;
Or any man now; like you; like me.
Time is so slow about whispering that it loves us—
Only at youth's end, shadow of the end.
We are not old; but time is, and tells us
Long before we die, in the middle of the field—
Where that hound was, trotting toward the river.
He knew, too. He didn't hear me laughing.
I was ungrown then; I was unlonely;
Time didn't love me. It loves you.

Another Pride

The father of the family, stoop-shouldered,
Has now another pride:
Not to mind much if his unspeakable authority
By smiles has died.

By laughter, even; he has learned to listen;
Secretly he basks
In the warm sun that wantons with his terrors,
Which time unmasks.

Which gray age has killed in him; he knows it,
And sometimes he sighs,
Wondering if this indifference be wisdom,
Or strength that dies.

The father of the family, forgiving,
Is himself forgiven;
But not for any sin, he thinks, wandering
That second heaven.

The Plague

"Little boy, what ails me, that you walk
So fearfully and far around?
You stare at this white hair
As at a ghost come out of ground.
I am not dead," the old man said;
And smiled, and frowned.

"Oh no, but it is catching, what you have."
He watched him from the windward side.
"I run like anyone;
I keep the distance good and wide."
So you ought, the old man thought,
And inly sighed.

Outly, though, he laughed and looked away.
"Little doctor, this disease—
You know it is but snow
And frosty blood and wits afreeze.
Yet not for you"—he searched him through—
"Save by degrees."

Envy the Old

Envy the young who have no words at all,
And the old, for they have had them. Now by wall
In sunshine, or by candle at the dance,
Or corner-warm, stillness is circumstance
Conclusive: there they sit, and no one says
They should be heedful of bright sentences.
Their silence, innocent of insult, tries
For how much truth? Who knows? It may be wise
Or sleepy, may be amorous of death
Or heavy with remembrance—the slow breath
Of sluggards at the goal. Who blames them here
For blinking? They are privileged to peer
Past us, past Him, past anyone at all,
And speak no word, those sitters by the wall.

Courage in Sons

Courage in sons, with wisdom's hesitation
Lest the good thing be lost, lest the far thing
That flutters be not seen, or seen too soon,
By dark, and so forgotten; justice, too,
Rejoicing (man's old music, heard again
Though every elder died); and even temperance,
Captain—by whose voice were these demanded,
Miracle past all? Not by the careful
Father's; or if so, not thence the cause.
Hope could not force it; asking might have marred,
O Providence, this prime result, this dream
Of none but generous gods. To whom, quietly,
Thanks for temperance, justice, wisdom, courage;
And to the generous sons that did receive them.

Startled, I Remember

Immensely the low sun
Paints all our city—shines
Prodigal on water towers;
Sweetens deep windows.

There it is, suddenly,
The soul of it: New York
Gold in the late day,
Dying and smiling.

Startled, I remember
Him that most loved this.
Where is he now, then?
Didn't I hear—

Oh, but the least—yes,
Certainly I felt it;
Mind and body turning, turning,
Trying to see.

Only as his would—
Once again, once again—
Oh, but he must sleep, though.
Let the night be.

In Memoriam

Look, till all of his years,
Foreshortened in your gaze,
Become, as under glass,
A few intensest days.

See? The courageous head—
The brown one—the white—
It flickers like a single
Star in densest night.

Listen. But no sound.
Not even glancing here.
The fever in him flashes:
The love against the fear.

Anxiety in this man
Yet could not kill the heart,
That now is burning coal,
And his immensest part.

The panic, the distress—
Oh, brothers, do not cry.
His love alone is climbing
The fences of the sky.

Epitaph

Let this be true, that I have loved
All men and things both here and gone;
But most the men whose love surpassed
My love, and so lives on and on.